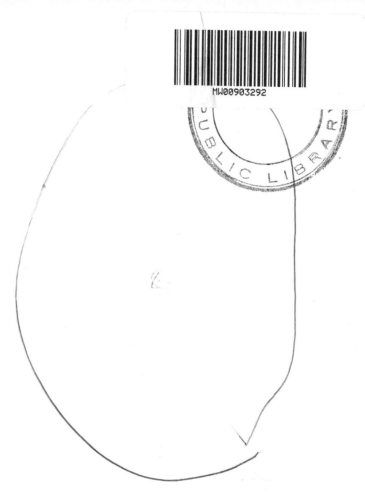

HOLIDAY COOKING
AROUND THE WORLD

Danish rice pudding can be eaten plain, with cinnamon, or with a raspberry glaze, as shown above. In Scandinavia, rice pudding is traditionally a Christmas and New Year's dish. (Recipe on page 47.)

HOLIDAY COOKING AROUND THE WORLD

PHOTOGRAPHS BY ROBERT L. AND DIANE WOLFE

easy menu
ethnic
cookbooks

Lerner Publications Company ▪ Minneapolis

Editor: Philip E. Baruth
Drawings by Jeanette Swofford

Additional photos courtesy of: p. 2, Burch Communications, Inc.; p. 10, Israel Ministry of Tourism; p. 11, Korea National Tourism Corporation; p. 44, RHODES Frozen Baking Dough. Photo p. 9 by Nancy Durrell McKenna.

Cover photos: lower left by Nancy Durrell McKenna; upper left, Robert L. and Diane Wolfe; upper right, RHODES Frozen Baking Dough; lower right by Jenny Matthews.

To Diane Fountain, Louise Silverstein, and Gladys Will—three of the world's premier cooks.

Libary of Congress Cataloging-in-Publication Data

Holiday Cooking Around the World.

(Easy menu ethnic cookbooks)
Includes index.
Summary: A collection of holiday recipes from fifteen different countries including a variety of dishes such as Thai egg rolls, Passover layer cake, paella, and Danish rice pudding.
1. Holiday cookery—Juvenile literature.
[1. Holiday cookery] I. Wolfe, Robert L., ill.
II. Wolfe, Diane, ill. III. Series.
TX739.H652 1988   641.5′68   88-8876
ISBN 0-8225-0922-9 (lib bdg.)

Manufactured in the United States of America

2 3 4 5 6 7 8 9 10 97 96 95 94 93 92 91 90 89

Desserts seem to stand for holidays worldwide.

CONTENTS

NORWAY
SOVIET UNION
EUROPE
ASIA
DENMARK
POLAND
ENGLAND
SPAIN
GREECE
LEBANON
KOREA
ISRAEL
NORTH AFRICA
AFRICA
VIETNAM
THAILAND
AUSTRALIA

NORTH AMERICA

MEXICO

CARIBBEAN ISLANDS

SOUTH AMERICA

INTRODUCTION

No matter what the reason for a holiday, or the weather while it is celebrated, food plays an essential part in the festivities. In the four months from December to March, the world celebrates some of the most sacred—and spectacular—of its holidays. For countries located far above the equator, these holidays fall in the heart of the winter. Days short on sunlight and long on rain and snow would be reason enough to gather with family.

But these months also mark important anniversaries, both religious and non-religious. Most of the world marks the beginning of a new year during this time. Jews celebrate the historic delivery of their people from slavery; Christians celebrate the birth of Christ. Countries to the far north stage festivals proclaiming kings and saints of winter, among them St. Nicholas (Holland) and Grandfather Frost (Russia). Peoples farther south throw open their doors and windows for rituals of cleansing and washing.

Holidays change and evolve over time. Climate, religion, and history all play major roles in the formation of each nation's celebrations. The Jewish holiday of Passover commemorates an actual historical event—the Exodus (escape) of Jews from Egypt in biblical times. Observation of this anniversary strengthens religious faith among today's Jewish families. And traditional Passover foods were chosen over the years from what the climate of the Middle East made available. The recipe in this book for chicken stuffed with oranges, an Israeli favorite, uses mainly citrus fruits and chicken. Both ingredients are abundant in Israel and acceptable to Jews who observe strictly the dietary laws of their faith.

The evolution of Christmas has also been guided by geography and culture. Christmas foods of northern countries are designed to warm guests and family. Hot chocolate, Yorkshire pudding, and Russian pirozhki are all warming to guests who have traveled to a gathering through the cold. In the Philippines, on the other hand, a favorite Christmas dessert is flan, or cold caramel custard. Desert dwellers, such as those in the Middle East and Africa, often prepare holiday desserts from nothing but simple, cold fresh fruit.

In many cases, the food a nation eats on a particular holiday has a more specific traditional or religious meaning. During the Jewish festival of Hanukkah, for instance, Israeli cooks serve many oil-fried foods, such as potato pancakes and doughnuts. The oil used in the frying, like the candelabra (menorah) that Jewish families light, commemorates the biblical miracle of a temple light burning eight days on a single day's supply of oil. As another example, the French often celebrate Christmas Eve with fresh goose. According to legend, the three wise men were met by geese at Christ's manger.

In other nations, and on other holidays, food simply represents good taste and love for family. Korean-born cook Okwha Chung remembers that nation's three-day festival of Sol as a time of pure celebration. "Sol is a time to greet the new year and to show respect for elders. My mother would serve many kinds of sweet and savory cakes, rice soup, egg rolls, meat dumplings, fried fish, broiled beef, kimchi, sweetened rice, candied lotus root and ginger, date balls, chestnut balls, and fresh fruit."

A family in Jerusalem prepares to share a festive meal. As they touch glasses, each person will say *L'chaim* — Hebrew for "To life."

Part of the idea behind any celebration is to have more than enough food and drink, to feed family and friends to the very fullest of your ability. In Poland, an extra place is set at the Christmas Eve table for unexpected guests — and the house is considered blessed should that place be filled by another hungry person. An old Polish proverb maintains that "a guest in the home is God in the home."

Another similarity among nations during holiday seasons is the attention devoted to gifts. Wrapped presents, both decorative and exciting to open, symbolize the holidays for many of us. Not surprisingly, many gift-giving traditions involve edible "packages" and presents. Most such traditions began before mass production made gifts and wrapping inexpensive enough to give so freely — food was very

Hot, dry regions—such as the Middle East and North Africa—grow a surprising amount of the world's produce. Celebrations in these areas always feature fresh fruit.

welcome as a special treat. In Puerto Rico, the leaves of plantains (a tropical fruit) are wrapped around a pork filling and tied up with a string. These "packages" are then boiled and served. Norwegians, during their Christmas Eve meal, serve a special rice pudding containing one whole almond. Whoever finds the almond in his or her portion is placed in charge of handing out gifts after the meal is over. Similarly, in Greece, a cake containing a small silver coin is served for New Year's Day. The prize winner is ensured of good luck for the coming year. Even in the United States, Christmas stockings—while now filled mostly with toys and trinkets—were originally stuffed with fruit, candy, and nuts.

A Holiday Smorgasbord

If you were to make a four-month tour of the world, boarding a fast jet in the middle of December, you would find festivals in progress almost any time or place that you landed. The week from the 25th of December to the 1st of January would be a busy one indeed. If your jet were fast enough, you could sample a traditional appetizer in one country and sit down to a holiday main dish in another, losing no more time in between than it takes to clear the plates. The recipes in this cookbook, which have been taken from 15 different countries, could be used to form just such a single, splendid holiday feast. If you prepare them all, you'll have a taste of the best the world has to offer on its most special days.

The Korean New Year celebration is known as Sol and lasts three days.

BEFORE YOU BEGIN

Cooking any dish, plain or fancy, is easier and more fun if you are familiar with its ingredients. The international dishes in this book make use of some ingredients you may not know. You should also be familiar with the special terms that will be used in these recipes. Therefore, *before* you start cooking, study the following "dictionary" of special ingredients and terms very carefully. Then read through the recipe you want to try from beginning to end.

Now you are ready to shop for ingredients and to organize the cookware you will need. Once you have assembled everything, you can begin to cook. It is also very important to read *The Careful Cook* on page 48 before you start. Following these rules will make your cooking experience safe, fun, and easy.

COOKING UTENSILS

colander—A bowl with holes in the bottom and sides. It is used for draining liquid from a solid food.

double boiler—A utensil made up of two pans that fit together. Heat from the water boiling in the lower pan cooks food in the upper pan without scorching.

fat thermometer—A special thermometer used for testing the temperature of hot fat for frying

paella pan—A shallow, two-handled skillet used to make and serve paella, Spain's national dish. (Any large skillet can be used in place of this pan.)

pastry brush – A small brush with nylon bristles used for coating food with melted butter or other liquids

rolling pin – A cylindrical tool used for rolling out dough

sieve – A hand-held device with very small holes or fine netting used for draining food or forcing small particles from larger pieces of food

slotted spoon – A spoon with small openings in the bowl. It is used to pick solid food out of a liquid.

spatula – A flat, thin utensil, usually metal, used to lift, toss, or scoop up food

tongs – A utensil used to grasp food

whisk – A small wire utensil used for beating foods by hand

wok – A pot with a rounded bottom and sloping sides, ideally suited for stir-fried dishes. A large skillet is a fine substitute.

COOKING TERMS

baste – To pour, brush, or spoon liquid over food as it cooks in order to flavor and moisten it

beat – To stir rapidly in a circular motion

braise – To cook slowly in a covered pot with liquid

broil – To cook food directly under a heat source so that the side facing the heat cooks rapidly

brown – To cook food quickly in fat over high heat so that the surface turns an even brown

fillet – A boneless piece of fish or meat

fold – To blend an ingredient with other ingredients by using a gentle overturning circular motion instead of by stirring or beating

garnish – To decorate with a small piece of food such as parsley

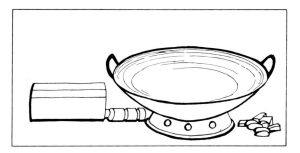

grate – To cut into tiny pieces by rubbing the food against a grater *knead* – To work dough by pressing it with palms, pushing it outward, and then pressing it over on itself

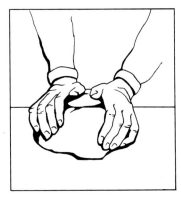

marinate – To soak food in a liquid in order to add flavor and to tenderize it

mince – To chop food into very small pieces

pinch – A very small amount, usually what you can pick up between your thumb and forefinger

preheat – To allow an oven or pan to warm up to a certain temperature before putting food in it

sauté – To fry quickly over high heat in oil or fat, stirring or turning the food to prevent burning

scald – To heat a liquid (such as milk) to a temperature just below its boiling point

shred – To tear or cut into small pieces, either by hand or with a grater

sift – To mix several dry ingredients together or to remove lumps in dry ingredients by putting them through a sieve or sifter

simmer – To cook over low heat in liquid kept just below its boiling point. Bubbles may occasionally rise to the surface.

stir-fry – To quickly cook bite-sized pieces of food in a small amount of oil over high heat

toss – To lightly mix pieces of food together

whip – To beat cream, gelatin, or egg white at high speed until light and fluffy in texture

SPECIAL INGREDIENTS

almond extract – A liquid made from the oil of the almond nut and used to give an almond flavor to food

bean sprouts – Sprouts from the mung bean. They can be bought either canned or fresh, or you can grow your own sprouts.

black mushrooms – Dried, fragrant mushrooms available at oriental groceries

cardamom seed – A spice from the ginger family, either whole or ground, that has a rich odor and gives food a sweet cool taste

cayenne pepper – Ground hot red pepper

cellophane noodles – Thin noodles made from mung beans

chorizo – A highly seasoned pork sausage

coriander seed – The seeds of an herb used both whole and ground to flavor foods

fish sauce – A bottled sauce made of processed fish, water, and salt. It is used widely in Vietnamese cooking and is an ingredient in the popular sauce *nuoc cham*. Fish sauce is available at Oriental groceries and some supermarkets.

garlic – An herb whose distinctive flavor is used in many dishes. Fresh garlic can usually be found in the produce department of a supermarket. Each piece or bulb can be broken up into several smaller sections called cloves. Most recipes use only one or two finely chopped cloves of this very strong herb. Before you

chop up a clove of garlic, you will have to remove the brittle, papery covering that surrounds it.

gelatin – A clear, powdered substance used as a thickening agent

halva – A sweet candy of crushed nuts or sesame seeds in honey syrup

lard – A solid shortening made from pork fat

lumpia – Thin skins made of flour, water, and coconut oil used as wrappers for egg rolls

matzo – Crisp unleavened bread eaten mainly at Passover by Jews around the world

olive oil – An oil made by pressing olives. It is used in cooking and for dressing salads.

oregano—The dried leaves, whole or powdered, of a rich and fragrant herb that is used as a seasoning in cooking

paprika—A red seasoning made from the ground dried pods of the *capsicum* pepper plant. It has a sweeter flavor than cayenne.

parsnip—The long, white, sweet-tasting root vegetable of the parsnip plant

pimento—Small, sweet red chilies that come in cans or bottles and are often used to add color to food. The word is sometimes spelled the Spanish way—*pimiento.*

poppy seed pastry filling—A thick, sweet mixture made from poppy seeds and corn syrup that is used in making pies, cakes, and breads

rice noodles—Long, very thin noodles made from rice

romaine lettuce—A lettuce with long, crisp, upright leaves

saffron—A deep orange, aromatic spice made from the flower of the saffron plant

sesame oil—The oil pressed from sesame seeds

This festive Polish table demonstrates the great care which the Polish people devote to holiday celebrations.

Shown above are several Lebanese staples—
kabobs, pita bread, and eggplant dip—with eggs
and beans, a Lenten dish. (Recipe on page 24.)

sesame seeds–Seeds from an herb grown in tropical countries. They are often toasted before they are eaten.

soy sauce–A dark brown sauce made from soybeans and other ingredients that is used to flavor oriental foods

sunflower oil–A cooking oil made from sunflower seeds

sweet-and-sour sauce–A sauce containing sugar and vinegar or lemon juice. Sweet-and-sour sauce can be purchased ready-made in most grocery stores.

turmeric–A yellow, aromatic spice made from the root of the turmeric plant

yeast–An ingredient used in baking that causes dough to rise up and become light. Yeast is available in cither small, white cakes (called compressed yeast) or in granular form (called active dry yeast).

AN INTERNATIONAL MENU

Below is a simplified menu for a varied, truly international holiday meal. The ethnic names of the dishes are given, along with a guide on how to pronounce them. At least one alternate for each stage of the meal is included. Desserts, as they seem universally to represent the holidays, receive special attention.

ENGLISH NAME	ETHNIC NAME/ PRONUNCIATION GUIDE	COUNTRY/HOLIDAY
Beverages		
Peanut Punch		Trinidad/All Festive Occasions
Ginger Beer		Tobago/All Festive Occasions
Appetizers		
Thai Egg Rolls	Poa Pee (pow pee-ah)	Thailand/New Year's Day
Eggs and Beans	Foul Mesdames (FOOL mah-DAHM)	Lebanon/Lent
Soups		
Asparagus Soup	Canh mang (cang mang)	Vietnam/New Year's Celebration
North African Chicken Soup	Marak Off Mizarahi (mah-RAHK OAF miz-rah-KHEE)	North Africa/Passover
Side Dishes		
Noodles with Poppy Seed	Kluski z makiem (KLOO-skih ZMAH-kyem)	Poland/Christmas Eve
Yorkshire Pudding		England/Christmas

Main Dishes

Pirozhki	Pirozhki (pee-ROZH-kee)	Russia/Any Holiday
Chicken Stuffed with Oranges	Off Memooleh Betapoozim (OAF meh-moo-LAY beh-tah-poo-ZEEM)	Israel/Passover
Simmered Beef Short Ribs	Kalbi jjim (kahl-bee jim)	Korea/New Year's Day
Paella	Paella (pah-EH-yuh)	Spain/Any Festive Occasion

Desserts

Butter Cookies	Kourabiéthes (koo-rah-BEETH-ehs)	Greece/Christmas
Passover Layer Cake	Ugat Matzot (oo-GHAT mah-TZOTE)	Israel/Passover
Christmas Bread	Julebrød (YOO-luh-broeh)	Norway/Christmas
Fried Pastry	Buñuelos/(boo-NYUE-lohs)	Mexico/Christmas
Danish Rice Pudding	Riskrem/(REES-krem)	Denmark/Christmas

The Norwegian design below (background) is an example of *rosemaling*, or rose-painting.

BEVERAGES

Caribbean beverages are served cold for the most part. On festive occasions, islanders from Trinidad and Tobago mix punches which make use of local spices, fruits, and food products. The two drinks listed below are simple, but they express the spirit of holidays in the Caribbean: stay cool.

Ginger Beer
Tobago

Recipe by Cheryl Kaufman

The sharp taste of ginger gives this drink a refreshingly different flavor.

¾ **cup (¼ pound) grated ginger root**
2 **tablespoons lime juice**
½ **teaspoon cream of tartar**
12 **cups (3 quarts) plus ¼ cup water**
2 **¼-ounce packages active dry yeast**
2 **cups sugar**

1. In a large bowl, combine grated ginger root, lime juice, and cream of tartar and stir well.
2. In a large kettle, bring 12 cups water to a boil over high heat. Carefully pour hot water over ginger mixture and set aside to cool.
3. In a small bowl, combine yeast, ¼ cup water, and ½ cup sugar. Stir to make a smooth paste.
4. When ginger mixture is lukewarm, add yeast mixture and stir well.
5. Cover bowl loosely with plastic wrap and let stand for 3 days.
6. Pour ginger mixture through a sieve into another large bowl underneath which catches the liquid.
7. Add remaining sugar to ginger beer and stir well. Serve chilled over ice.

Makes 3 quarts

Peanut Punch
Trinidad

Recipe by Cheryl Kaufman

This thick, rich drink is easy to make and very filling.

½ to ⅔ cup smooth peanut butter
3 cups cold whole milk
4 tablespoons sugar
   dash cinnamon
   dash nutmeg

1. Place all ingredients in a blender and blend on high speed for about 30 seconds or until thick and frothy.
2. Pour into glasses and serve immediately.
Serves 4

Ginger beer and peanut punch are served to guests on many Caribbean holidays.

Hearty Thai egg rolls, shown here with traditional _nam pla prig_ sauce, have become popular year-round in the United States.

APPETIZERS

As most holidays are all-day affairs, the appetizer becomes an important addition to the meal plan. For the choices listed below, we move across the Atlantic Ocean to both the Far and the Middle East. Lebanese and Thai appetizers have this in common: they can both easily be eaten as a meal in themselves.

Thai Egg Rolls (Poa Pee)
Thailand

Recipe by Supenn Harrison and Judy Monroe

Thai egg rolls are usually served on New Year's with foods like whole chicken marinated in sugar and soy sauce, steamed tofu, and Thai coconut custard. Although the Thai use delicate rice paper for their egg rolls, we suggest that you use lumpia papers, a thin flour-and-water wrapper. Look for lumpia in oriental groceries or in *the gourmet frozen foods section of your supermarket.*

3 black mushrooms
3½ ounces (one-half package) rice noodles or cellophane noodles
1 egg
½ pound ground pork
½ pound ground beef
1 cup peeled and shredded carrots
1 cup bean sprouts or 1 cup shredded cabbage
½ medium onion, chopped
1 tablespoon fish sauce
¼ tablespoon pepper
½ clove garlic, finely chopped
1 teaspoon sugar
16-ounce package lumpia, thawed (about 25 wrappers)
½ cup vegetable oil
sweet-and-sour sauce

1. In a small bowl, soak black mushrooms in hot water for 15 minutes. Drain well in a colander and shred, discarding the stems.
2. Soak noodles in hot water according to package directions. When soft, drain and cut into 2-inch lengths with a sharp knife or scissors.
3. In a large bowl, beat egg well. Add black mushrooms, noodles, pork, beef, carrots, bean sprouts, onion, fish sauce, pepper, garlic, and sugar. Mix well.
4. Place 1 wrapper on a flat surface. Cover remaining wrappers with a slightly damp kitchen towel so they don't dry out. Roll up according to directions on page 24.
5. In a large skillet or wok, heat oil over medium heat for 1 minute. Carefully place 3 rolls in oil and fry slowly for about 10 minutes or until golden brown. Turn and fry other side 10 minutes. Keep fried rolls warm in a 200° oven.
6. Cut each egg roll into 4 pieces. Serve hot with individual bowls of sweet and sour sauce.

Makes 25 egg rolls

HOW TO WRAP EGG ROLLS

1. Have ready 1 beaten egg and a pastry brush.

2. Place about 1½ tablespoons of filling mixture just below center of skin.

3. Fold bottom edge over filling.

4. Fold in the two opposite edges so that they overlap.

5. Brush top edge corner with beaten egg. Roll up toward top edge and press edge to seal. Repeat with remaining wrappers.

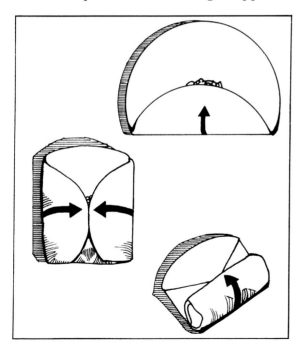

Eggs and Beans (Foul Mesdames) Lebanon

Recipe by Suad Amari

Traditionally made during Lent, this nourishing, meatless dish is often eaten as a main course, especially in poorer households. More often, however, it is eaten as an appetizer accompanying main dishes like garlic chicken and tabbouleh (a cracked wheat salad). Canned kidney or pinto beans will work as well in this recipe as the Egyptian field beans which the Lebanese prefer.

2 15-ounce cans of beans, undrained
2 cloves garlic, peeled and finely chopped
2 tablespoons olive oil
  juice of 1 lemon (about 3 tablespoons)
1 teaspoon salt
¼ teaspoon pepper
4 hard-cooked eggs, quartered

**4 tablespoons chopped parsley
for garnish**

1. In a large saucepan, combine beans and their liquid with garlic, olive oil, and lemon juice. Add salt and pepper and mix well. Simmer over medium heat, stirring occasionally, about 10 to 15 minutes or until heated.
2. Pour beans into individual bowls. Arrange hard-cooked egg pieces on top of each bowl, sprinkle with parsley, and serve.

Serves 4

SOUPS

The soups below demonstrate how easily regional foods and dishes pass from country to country. Asparagus was brought to Vietnam by the French and quickly became a very popular vegetable. The Vietnamese now call asparagus "Western bamboo." Similarly, North African chicken soup has been made popular in Israel by North African Jewish immigrants. Both soups are holiday favorites.

Asparagus Soup (Canh mang) Vietnam

Recipe by Chi Nguyen and Judy Monroe

This soup would ordinarily be served for New Year's dinner with stir-fried vegetables and roast suckling pig. Asparagus soup is also delicious when made with broccoli, cauliflower, brussels sprouts, or peas.

**1 egg
2 tablespoons cornstarch
¼ cup water
2 10¾-ounce cans (about 3 cups)
    chicken broth
½ pound fresh asparagus, cut into bite-
    size pieces or 1 10-ounce package
    frozen chopped asparagus, thawed
1 whole chicken breast, skinned, boned,
    and cut into bite-size pieces
2 teaspoons fish sauce**

1. Beat egg in a small bowl. Set aside.
2. In another small bowl, mix cornstarch and water to make a paste. Set aside.
3. In a large saucepan, bring broth to a boil over high heat. Add asparagus and reduce heat to medium. Cover and cook for 3 minutes or until crisp-tender.
4. Add chicken. Cook for 3 to 4 minutes or until chicken and asparagus are thoroughly cooked.
5. Add fish sauce and cornstarch paste. (If cornstarch has started to separate from the water, stir well before adding.) Stir well about 1 to 2 minutes or until soup starts to thicken.
6. Add beaten egg a little at a time, stirring constantly. Cook for 30 seconds.
7. Serve hot over rice, or in individual soup bowls with rice on the side.

Serves 4

Asparagus soup can be prepared with broccoli, cauliflower, or peas and is both colorful and filling.

North African Chicken Soup (Marak Off Mizarahi) North Africa

Recipe by Josephine Bacon

This tangy, lemony, peppery soup is prepared for Passover in North Africa. If the chicken meat is eaten separately, it is eaten with rice, as North African Sephardic Jews are allowed to eat rice on Passover. (The Jews of German origin, called Ashkenazim, are forbidden rice on Passover.)

1 **large chicken (at least 3 pounds)**
3 **lemons**
2 **small turnips, peeled**
3 **onions, peeled (1 stuck with 2 whole cloves)**
2 **carrots, peeled and sliced lengthwise**
1 **bunch parsley, with root if possible, or 1 small parsnip, peeled, or both**
2 **teaspoons salt**
½ **teaspoon pepper**
1 **teaspoon cinnamon**
1 **teaspoon chili powder**
¼ **teaspoon powdered saffron or turmeric**
2 **eggs, beaten**

1. Wash chicken. Squeeze juice from one of the lemons into a small bowl and set aside. Rub chicken all over with the inside of a squeezed lemon half. Place chicken in a large, deep kettle and add enough water to barely cover it.
2. Bring water in kettle to a boil over high heat. With a spoon, skim off the foam that forms on the surface of the water.
3. When you have removed as much foam as possible and the water is boiling, reduce heat and add vegetables, parsley, salt, and pepper. Cover kettle and let chicken simmer 1 hour.
4. Add lemon juice and remaining spices to soup. Cover kettle and simmer for another hour.
5. With tongs, carefully remove chicken from pot. Place on a plate and let cool. When cool, remove meat from bones and set aside.

6. Carefully pour broth through a sieve into another large pan placed underneath to catch the liquid. Save the vegetables.

7. Cool broth to room temperature, then refrigerate for 30 minutes to bring fat to the surface. Skim the surface with a paper towel to absorb fat.

8. Before serving, beat eggs into 1 cup of the soup and return to kettle. Add the cooked vegetables and, if desired, bite-size pieces of the cooked chicken. (The chicken can also be served separately.) Reheat soup, stirring occasionally. Do not let it boil.

9. Serve soup hot with remaining lemon cut into wedges for squeezing into soup.

Serves 6 to 8

Chicken soup has a very special place in Jewish societies from North Africa to the United States.

SIDE DISHES

Holiday side dishes, even more than appetizers, can sometimes stand in place of main dishes. For that reason, we have selected side dishes that are always served as accompaniments to the main course. Yorkshire pudding, for instance, traditionally stands beside roast beef on an English table. Noodles with poppy seed, a Polish favorite, is just one of 21 other courses served on Christmas Eve after a day of fasting.

Yorkshire Pudding
England

Recipe by Barbara Hill

A British pudding is not always a sweet dessert. Yorkshire pudding has a light, fluffy batter and is often served with horseradish sauce.

½ cup all-purpose flour
1 teaspoon baking powder
¼ teaspoon salt
pinch of pepper
1 egg
1 cup milk
2 tablespoons lard or vegetable shortening or beef drippings
¼ cup cold water

1. In a bowl, sift flour and baking powder.
2. Mix in salt and pepper.
3. Make a hollow in the center of flour mixture and crack egg into it. Stir well.
4. Add milk gradually and beat until smooth, using an electric mixer if available.
5. Refrigerate batter at least one-half hour.
6. One-half hour before the meal is to be served, heat the oven to 425°. Move meat to a low shelf in the oven, where the temperature will stay slightly cooler.
7. Put lard in an 8- by 12-inch baking pan and melt the lard on top shelf of oven. Or have an experienced cook help you draw 2 tablespoons of fat from the roasting pan and place it in the 8- by 12-inch pan.
8. Pour ¼ cup cold water onto chilled pudding batter and stir well. Then pour mixture into melted lard in the baking

pan. Return pan to the top shelf of the oven for 20 minutes.

9. Cut Yorkshire pudding into squares and arrange them around roast sirloin with roast potatoes. Serve with horseradish sauce, if desired.

Serves 4

Noodles with Poppy Seed (Kluski z makiem) Poland

Recipe by Danuta Zamojska-Hutchins

Because of the abundance of poppies in Poland, poppy seeds are used in many different foods. This particular dish is eaten only on the night before Christmas.

1 16-ounce package shell or ribbon macaroni, cooked
1 12½-ounce can Solo® poppy seed pastry filling
4 tablespoons honey
1 cup heavy cream or half and half
½ cup golden raisins
2 tablespoons butter or margarine

No Polish Christmas Eve would be complete without a dish of noodles with poppy seed.

1. Cook noodles according to directions on package.

2. Meanwhile, combine poppy seed filling, honey, and cream in a mixing bowl and stir until smooth. Stir in raisins.

3. Melt butter in double boiler. Add poppy seed mixture and heat thoroughly.

4. Pour poppy seed mixture over hot, drained noodles and serve immediately.

Serves 10 to 12

MAIN DISHES

Main dishes are, if not the most important part, then at least the most visible part of a holiday feast. Cooks of all nations work hard to assure that their main course makes attractive use of the finest available meats and seafoods. Spanish cooks combine both to produce paella, their national dish. In Russia, meat is rolled inside dough and baked to form pirozhki. Koreans simmer beef to increase its tenderness and, perhaps, to prolong the anticipation of the guests.

A sharp knife is best for mincing or chopping food, but remember to be careful when using it.

Pirozhki
Russia

Recipe by Gregory Plotkin

This substantial meat pastry is sometimes served with straw potatoes and vegetable salad. At Christmas time, however, pirozhki is more often served with hot borsch (a beet soup) and caviar.

Filling:
- 4 tablespoons sunflower oil
- 3 medium onions, peeled and chopped
- 1½ pounds ground beef
- 1 teaspoon salt
- ⅛ teaspoon pepper

1. In a large frying pan, heat 2 tablespoons oil over medium-high heat for 1 minute. Add onions and sauté until golden brown. Remove from pan and set aside.
2. Add remaining oil to pan and heat for 1 minute over medium-high heat. Add meat and cook until brown, mashing with a

fork to break into small pieces. Drain off fat.

3. Place meat, onions, salt, and pepper in a blender. Cover and blend on maximum speed for 5 to 7 seconds. (If you don't have a blender, place meat in a large bowl and mash well with a fork.)

Dough:
2 cups all-purpose flour
⅛ teaspoon salt
1 egg
½ to ¾ cup water or skim milk
   melted butter

1. In a medium bowl, mix flour, salt, and egg. Add liquid, a little at a time, until dough is stiff.
2. Knead dough for 2-4 minutes on a floured surface. (You will have to add more flour.) Roll out dough to ⅛-inch thickness with a rolling pin. With a glass or cookie cutter, cut out rounds of dough 3 inches in diameter.
3. Preheat oven to 400°.
4. Put 1 tablespoon filling on one half of each circle. Moisten edges of dough with a little water. Fold dough over filling and press edges together first with your fingers, then with the tines of a fork.
5. Place pirozhki on a greased cookie sheet and bake for 30 minutes or until golden brown. Brush with melted butter and serve at room temperature.

Makes 12 to 18 pirozhki

Russian pirozhki (front) might share space on a holiday table with straw potatoes (left) and vegetable salad (right).

Chicken Stuffed with Oranges (Off Memooleh Betapoozim) Israel

Recipe by Josephine Bacon

This is an adaptation of a prize-winning recipe from a contest organized by the Israeli Touring Club in Jerusalem many years ago. This dish, during Passover, is eaten with matzo and melon.

1 2½- to 3-pound chicken
1 lemon
2 teaspoons salt
1 teaspoon garlic powder
2 teaspoons paprika
1 teaspoon chili powder
1 teaspoon ground coriander
2 oranges
1 cup water
2 onions, peeled

Fresh citrus provides a special accent to chicken.

1. Preheat oven to 425°.
2. Rinse chicken inside and out under cold running water. Pat dry with paper towels.
3. Place chicken in a roasting pan. Cut lemon in half and rub one half over surface of chicken.
4. In a small bowl, mix spices together and sprinkle over chicken.
5. Squeeze juice from lemon half and from 1 of the oranges into roasting pan and add water. Place remaining orange, whole and unpeeled, in chicken cavity. Cut onions in half and add to pan.
6. Cook chicken for 15 minutes, then baste with the pan juices and lower heat to 350°. Cook for 1 hour, basting after 30 minutes.
7. Remove orange from cavity of chicken. Cut orange and onions into small pieces and serve with chicken.

Serves 4 to 6

Simmered Beef Short Ribs (Kalbi jjim) Korea

Recipe by Okwha Chung and Judy Monroe

In Korea, simmering and steaming are the most popular ways to cook meat. This beef dish, in addition to being served during the three-day New Year's celebration, is also popular on birthdays. One would normally serve kimchi (a spicy fermented cabbage) and possibly cucumber soup with this filling entree.

½ **cup water**
2½ **pounds lean beef short ribs, separated into pieces**
½ **cup soy sauce**
2 **teaspoons sesame oil**
¼ **cup sugar**
½ **teaspoon black pepper**
1 **clove garlic, peeled and chopped**
1 **small onion, peeled and chopped**
2 **large carrots, peeled and chopped**

3½   teaspoons toasted sesame seeds
3   green onions, finely chopped
5   mushrooms, cut in half

1. Combine water and meat in a large saucepan and bring to a boil over high heat. Reduce heat to medium, cover, and cook, stirring occasionally, for 1½ hours or until meat is tender.
2. Add soy sauce, sesame oil, sugar, black pepper, garlic, onions, carrots, and sesame seeds and stir well. Cover, reduce heat to low, and cook about 30 minutes or until vegetables are tender.
3. Add green onions and mushrooms and cook 1 to 2 minutes more.
4. Garnish with remaining sesame seeds.

Serves 4

Paella
Spain

Recipe by Rebecca Christian

"Paella" has no English translation. Spain's national dish, paella takes its name from the shallow, two-handled black skillet—called a paella pan—in which it is made. This pan is taken from the stove and placed directly on the table and might be accompanied by lentil soup and stewed vegetables, with caramel custard for dessert.

12 small fresh clams in shells or ½ cup canned cooked clams
12 medium-sized fresh shrimp in shells or ½ cup canned cooked shrimp
8 ounces chorizo or other garlic-seasoned sausage
2 tablespoons olive or cooking oil
   a 2½-pound chicken, cut into 8 serving pieces
2 15-ounce cans (about 4 cups) chicken broth
1 medium-sized onion, cut into wedges
1 sweet red or green pepper, cleaned

**out and cut into strips, or 1 canned
whole pimento, drained and sliced**
½ **teaspoon minced garlic**
 2 **cups white rice, uncooked**
½ **teaspoon oregano**
¼ **teaspoon saffron**
½ **cup fresh peas or ½ 10-ounce
package frozen peas**

1. *For fresh clams*—cover clams in shells with salted water using 3 tablespoons salt to 8 cups cold water. Let stand 15 minutes and rinse. Repeat soaking and rinsing twice. Set aside. *For fresh shrimp*—remove shells from shrimp. Split each shrimp down the back with a small knife and pull out the black or white vein. Rinse shrimp and dry on paper towels. Set aside.
2. In a paella pan or a very wide skillet, cook sausage 10 minutes or until done. Drain, let cool, and slice. Set aside.
3. Heat oil in the skillet and brown chicken 15 minutes, turning occasionally. Remove chicken and set aside.
4. In a saucepan, heat chicken broth to a boil. Meanwhile, brown onion, red pepper, and garlic in oil remaining in the skillet. Remove oven racks and preheat the oven to 400°.
5. Add rice, boiling broth, oregano, and saffron to the skillet. Bring to a boil over high heat and then remove.
6. Arrange chicken, sausage, shrimp, and clams on top of rice. Scatter peas over all. Set the pan on the oven floor and bake uncovered for 25 to 30 minutes or until liquid has been absorbed by rice. *Never stir paella after it goes into the oven.*
7. Remove paella from the oven and cover with a kitchen towel. Let rest 5 minutes. Serve at the table directly from the pan.
Serves 6

Paella, a Spanish national dish, is served on most festive occasions and takes full advantage of Spain's bountiful seafood catch.

DESSERTS

While desserts often come first to our minds when we think of holiday cooking, many holidays involve religious laws against popular treats. Catholics, for instance, are asked to give up a certain favorite habit or food during Lent to show respect and discipline during this holiday. Many swear off sweets, especially chocolate. Jews during Passover are forbidden to eat leavened foods (mostly those that use yeast or baking powder—most breads, cakes, cookies, etc.). The following desserts are all sweet and delicious, although, because of their different origins, they use different sweeteners and basic ingredients.

Butter Cookies (Kourabiéthes) Greece

Recipe by Lynne Villios

Butter cookies are very popular year-round in Greece. At Christmas time, they are topped with whole cloves to symbolize the spices brought by the three wise men.

2½ cups all-purpose flour
1 teaspoon baking powder
¼ teaspoon salt
1 cup (2 sticks) butter, softened
½ cup sugar
1 egg
½ teaspoon vanilla extract
¼ teaspoon almond extract
powdered sugar for sprinkling

1. Preheat oven to 350°.
2. In a small bowl, combine flour, baking powder, and salt.
3. In a large bowl, beat together butter, sugar, and egg until light and fluffy. Add

flour mixture to butter mixture and mix until well blended. Add vanilla and almond extracts and mix well.

4. With your hands, form dough, about ½ tablespoon at a time, into balls, crescents, or S-shapes.

5. Place cookies 2 inches apart on cookie sheet. Put on middle oven rack and bake 15 to 18 minutes or until barely brown around the edges.

6. Remove from cookie sheet with spatula and cool on wire rack for 5 minutes.

7. With a flour sifter, sift powdered sugar over cookies.

Makes about 3 dozen cookies

Greek butter cookies are eaten year-round but are especially welcome at Christmas time.

Passover Matzo Layer Cake (Ugat Matzot) Israel

Recipe by Josephine Bacon

The halva used in this recipe is a sticky-sweet candy—a hard block of ground nuts mixed with sugar and honey. The best halva is made from almonds, but you can also buy sesame and peanut halva. Halva can be purchased at any Greek, Middle Eastern, or Jewish market.

6 tablespoons sugar
4 squares unsweetened chocolate
1 cup water
1 stick (¼ pound) butter or margarine, cut into pieces
6 ounces halva, cut into small pieces
2 tablespoons cornstarch
6 large matzos
colored candy sprinkles for decoration

1. In a medium saucepan, combine sugar, chocolate, and water. Cook over medium-high heat, stirring constantly, until chocolate is completely melted and mixture comes to a boil.

2. Add butter and halva. Continue stirring until mixture boils again, then remove pan from the heat.

3. In a small bowl, mix cornstarch with 2 tablespoons water and stir into chocolate mixture. Cook over medium heat, stirring until mixture thickens. Remove pan from heat.

4. Put 1 matzo on a platter large enough to let it lie flat. Spread an even layer of chocolate mixture over matzo. Place another matzo on top and cover with more of the chocolate mixture. Repeat with remaining matzos, finishing with a layer of chocolate. Scatter sprinkles over cake for decoration.

5. Refrigerate cake overnight so chocolate mixture will harden and flavors will mingle. To serve, cut cake with a sharp knife into 1- by 2-inch rectangles.

Serves 10

During Passover, matzo cake is often served with melon.

Christmas Bread (Julebrød)
Norway

Recipe by Sylvia Munsen

Norwegian Christmas bread makes wonderful toast. For that reason, it often serves as a breakfast dish, sharing space on the table with rice porridge and soft-boiled eggs.

2 tablespoons active dry yeast
1 tablespoon sugar
¼ cup warm water
2 cups milk
½ cup shortening
½ cup sugar
2 teaspoons salt
2 teaspoons ground cardamom seed
6½ cups all-purpose flour
1 cup candied red and green cherries
　　or assorted candied fruit, cut
　　in thirds
1 cup raisins
½ cup blanched almonds, finely chopped

additional all-purpose flour
　(½ to 1½ cups)

1. Soften raisins by putting them in a small amount of hot water. Prepare cherries by shaking them in a bag with a little flour. Set cherries and raisins aside.
2. In a glass measuring cup or a drinking glass, dissolve yeast and 1 tablespoon sugar in ¼ cup warm water.
3. In a saucepan, scald milk. Stir in shortening and let cool for 15 minutes.
4. When milk and shortening have cooled, pour into a big mixing bowl.
5. Add ½ cup sugar, salt, and ground cardamom seed to milk and shortening. Stir.
6. With a mixing spoon, stir in 2 cups flour, 1 cup at a time.
7. Add yeast, sugar, and water mixture. Stir.
8. Stir in 2 more cups flour. Then add candied fruit, raisins, and chopped almonds, mixing well.
9. Stir in 2½ cups of remaining flour, 1 cup at a time.
10. Turn dough out on a floured board

and knead well. Use as much remaining flour as it takes to produce a springy, elastic texture. (See kneading diagram.) Place dough in a greased bowl and cover with a damp cloth.

11. Put dough in a warm place (about 80°) or in a closed oven (turned off) with a pan of hot water on the bottom rack. Let dough rise until double. Punch down and let rise until double again.

12. Punch down and cut into 2 equal sections.

13. Knead well. Form round loaves and place them on a cookie sheet. Cover with a damp cloth and let rise in a warm place.

14. Preheat the oven to 350°. (Be sure to remove the 2 loaves first if you have put them in the oven to rise!)

15. Bake loaves for about 35 minutes. (Tops should be golden brown.)

16. Drip glaze onto loaves after they cool.

Makes 2 round loaves

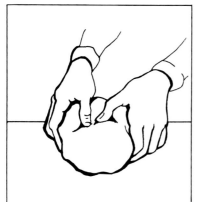 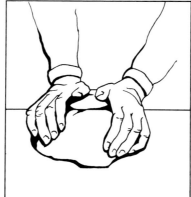 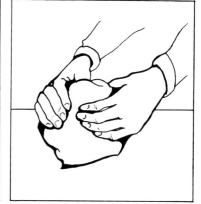

1. Form dough into a ball. 2. Press dough down with your palms. Then push it outward with the heel of your hand. 3. Fold and press dough over on itself. 4. Repeat Step 2, pressing dough down and pushing it outward.

Christmas bread makes a colorful holiday gift. For an extra festive touch, frost the loaves with white icing and decorate with sliced almonds.

Christmas Bread Glaze

2 cups powdered sugar
1 egg white, lightly beaten
½ teaspoon lemon juice
¼ to ½ cup water

1. Sift powdered sugar into a medium mixing bowl. Make a well in center of sugar and pour egg white and lemon juice into it. Gradually mix powdered sugar into liquid with a spoon, adding water little by little until frosting is smooth. (Frosting should be thick enough to coat the back of a spoon.)
2. When completely smooth, pour frosting over loaves, letting it dribble over the sides.

Fried Pastry
(Buñuelos)
Mexico

Recipe by Rosa Coronado

On Christmas Eve, Mexican street vendors sell buñuelos in the town plazas, handing them to customers on pottery dishes that have cracks or flaws in them. After eating the pastries, the people throw the dishes on the ground and break them. This custom may be connected to ancient Indian ceremonies celebrating the end of the old year and the beginning of a new one.

4 cups all-purpose flour
2 tablespoons sugar
1 tablespoon baking powder
2 eggs
2 tablespoons milk
¼ cup vegetable oil
1 cup warm water
1 cup vegetable oil (for frying)
½ cup sugar
3 tablespoons cinnamon

1. Thoroughly mix flour, sugar, and baking powder in a large bowl.
2. In another bowl, beat together eggs and milk. Then add to dry ingredients. Stir in ¼ cup oil and mix well.
3. Add warm water and mix until dough can be handled easily. (If dough is too

dry, add a few more teaspoons of warm water, one at a time.)

4. Place dough on a lightly floured board and knead until smooth.

5. Divide dough into 20 to 24 pieces and shape each into a ball. Flatten balls on the board with the palm of your hand. Cover with a cloth for 20 minutes.

6. On a lightly floured board, roll out each flattened ball with a rolling pin into a large round shape about 6 or 7 inches in diameter. Let stand for about 5 minutes.

7. Heat 1 cup oil in an electric frying pan set to 360°. (If you don't have an electric frying pan, use a fat thermometer to check the temperature of oil heated in a regular frying pan.) Just before frying, stretch each buñuelo a little more by hand.

8. Fry each buñuelo until underside is golden brown (about 3 minutes). Turn and fry other side until crisp. Remove and drain on a paper towel.

9. In a small bowl, combine sugar and cinnamon. Sprinkle hot buñuelos with cinnamon and sugar mixture.

Makes 20 to 24

Mexican fried pastry proves that holiday treats can be simple as well as delicious.

Danish Rice Pudding (Riskrem)
Denmark

Recipe by Sylvia Munsen

Denmark and its two closest neighbors—Norway and Sweden—each have their own version of holiday rice pudding. The Danes usually serve their pudding with raspberry sauce, a colorful addition to a holiday table.

2 **envelopes unflavored gelatin**
½ **cup sugar**
½ **cup water**
½ **teaspoon salt**
2 **cups milk**
1½ **cups cooked white rice**
2 **teaspoons vanilla extract**
¼ **cup chopped almonds**
1 **cup chilled whipping cream**

1. In a saucepan, heat gelatin, sugar, water, and salt. Stir constantly until gelatin is dissolved (about 1 minute).
2. Stir in milk, rice, vanilla, and almonds.
3. Place the saucepan in a bowl of ice water, stirring occasionally for about 15 minutes. (Mixture should form a slight lump when dropped from a spoon.)
4. Beat whipping cream until stiff and fold into rice mixture.
5. Pour into an ungreased 1½-quart mold. Cover and chill until set (about 3 hours).
6. Turn out and serve cold with raspberry sauce.

Serves 8

Raspberry Sauce:

1 **10-ounce package frozen raspberries, thawed**
½ **cup apple or currant jelly**
1 **tablespoon cold water**
1½ **teaspoons cornstarch**

1. In a saucepan, bring raspberries (with syrup) and jelly to a boil.
2. Combine water and cornstarch in a bowl. Then stir into raspberries.
3. Bring to a boil again, stirring constantly.
4. Boil and stir for one minute.
5. Serve warm sauce on top of cold pudding.

THE CAREFUL COOK

Whenever you cook, there are certain safety rules you must always keep in mind. Even experienced cooks follow these rules when they are in the kitchen.

1. Always wash your hands before handling food.
2. Thoroughly wash all raw vegetables and fruits to remove dirt, chemicals, and insecticides.
3. Use a cutting board when cutting up vegetables and fruits. Don't cut them up in your hand! And be sure to cut in a direction *away* from you and your fingers.
4. Long hair or loose clothing can easily catch fire if brought near the burners of the stove. If you have long hair, tie it back before you start cooking.
5. Turn all pot handles toward the back of the stove so that you will not catch your sleeve or jewelry on them. This is especially important when younger brothers and sisters are around. They could easily knock off a pot and get burned.

6. Always use a pot holder to steady hot pots or to take pans out of the oven. Don't use a wet cloth on a hot pan because the steam it produces could burn you.
7. Lift the lid of a steaming pot with the opening away from you so that you will not get burned.
8. If you do get burned, hold the burn under cold running water. Do not put grease or butter on it. Cold water helps to take the heat out, but grease or butter will only keep it in.
9. If grease or cooking oil catches fire, throw baking soda or salt at the bottom of the flame to put it out. (Water will *not* put out a grease fire.) Call for help and try to turn all the stove burners to "off."

METRIC CONVERSION CHART

WHEN YOU KNOW		MULTIPLY BY	TO FIND	
MASS (weight)				
ounces	(oz)	28.0	grams	(g)
pounds	(lb)	0.45	kilograms	(kg)
VOLUME				
teaspoons	(tsp)	5.0	milliliters	(ml)
tablespoons	(Tbsp)	15.0	milliliters	
fluid ounces	(oz)	30.0	milliliters	
cup	(c)	0.24	liters	(l)
pint	(pt)	0.47	liters	
quart	(qt)	0.95	liters	
gallon	(gal)	3.8	liters	
TEMPERATURE				
Fahrenheit	(°F) temperature	5/9 (after subtracting 32)	Celsius	(°C) temperature

COMMON MEASURES AND THEIR EQUIVALENTS

3 teaspoons = 1 tablespoon

8 tablespoons = ½ cup

2 cups = 1 pint

2 pints = 1 quart

4 quarts = 1 gallon

16 ounces = 1 pound

INDEX

Simmered beef short ribs (back) are a colorful addition to a New Year's feast. Simmered chicken (front) is equally appetizing.

Cooking the **AFRICAN** Way
Cooking the **CARIBBEAN** Way
Cooking the **CHINESE** Way
Cooking the **ENGLISH** Way
Cooking the **FRENCH** Way
Cooking the **GERMAN** Way
Cooking the **GREEK** Way
Cooking the **HUNGARIAN** Way
Cooking the **INDIAN** Way
Cooking the **ISRAELI** Way
Cooking the **ITALIAN** Way
Cooking the **JAPANESE** Way
Cooking the **KOREAN** Way
Cooking the **LEBANESE** Way
Cooking the **MEXICAN** Way
Cooking the **NORWEGIAN** Way
Cooking the **POLISH** Way
Cooking the **RUSSIAN** Way
Cooking the **SPANISH** Way
Cooking the **THAI** Way
Cooking the **VIETNAMESE** Way

No matter where on the earth we live, no matter why or how we celebrate, our festivals all come to the same end: empty plates and bright memories.